This book belongs to:

____

Made in the USA
Monee, IL
16 December 2022

22348351R00066